Christabel Lancing has a Masters degree with Honours in History of Art from The University of Glasgow. She is also a graduate journalist from the University of London. She has published in The Herald Scotland, worked for Haymarket Publishing and has undertaken research for the acclaimed investigative journalist and author Mark Hollingsworth.

Christabel is a certified teacher of both English as a Foreign Language and Business English. She has written and produced new English learning and marketing materials.

19th Century French literature is Lancing's favourite genre and she has a deep interest in art history and painting. Her passion is singing, playing and writing music. She was a member of the world-famous Huddersfield Choral Society for several years before recently moving back to London.

This book is dedicated to two people: my son, Sam, who I hope will grow up with the ability to express himself freely in a world where we still learn to keep our emotions under wraps, and my great grandmother, Bluebell Matilda Hunter.

Bluebell was better known in the literary world by her pen names, George Lancing, Boris M. Hunter and John Guildford as a novelist and serial writer, at a time when it was difficult to be published as a female author.

Born in 1877, Bluebell Hunter was a daughter of G.D Williams, the first Chief Editor of Reuters. She made her mark as an author of significant standing and enjoyed friendships with W.B Yeats and H.G Wells.

I mention my grandfather, Thomas Martin. My poetry has been stimulated, hugely, by him. His expressions were couched in his own environment – an Irish Linen Border village. Though his work was never published, except in local newspapers, I have often reached for these poems on a winter Sunday evening sitting by the open fire, and have been comforted by his empathetic style and vision of hope.

My dear friends, Audra, Dan and Asmita encouraged me to express my creative spirit in this uninhibited way at a time when I was at a low ebb. They were my driving lodestar.

Christabel Lancing

BESIDE A STRANGER

AUSTIN MACAULEY PUBLISHERS™

LONDON • CAMBRIDGE • NEW YORK • SHARJAH

A CIP catalogue record for this title is available from the British Library.

ISBN 9781035839025 (Paperback)
ISBN 9781035839032 (ePub e-book)

www.austinmacauley.com

First Published 2024
Austin Macauley Publishers Ltd®
1 Canada Square
Canary Wharf
London
E145AA

20240503

I would like to give thanks to Austin Macauley Publishers for providing me with the opportunity to be published as a debut author.

Beside a Stranger

How can I miss you when I don't even know you?
Why's it important, even when you're not there, how can I
have it when I can't even show you,
When can I feel it if you really can't care?

The figment that's you; the shadow that's me,
The hope that one day I'll just walk into thee,
There won't be a sound, or a flutter in th'air, just the
knowing our love is softly laid bare.

...

Neutered Heart

Where did that time go when you used to hold my hand,
Walking through the park or listening to a band?

The deafening silence of your heart's intention,
Makes mine redundant, not to mention
The look, the smile, that knowing gaze
That shone my heart in a thousand rays.

…

Au Revoir

Did you realise I meant it when I said goodbye,
The clock's watching over, no time to bide,
Could I say I'll miss you more than I'll ever deny?
Those blissful nights, Oh! How I'll cry.

We must remember the heart doesn't lie,
I'll feel you forever in the dark night sky,
Bruised and watchful, tears shed and shy,
Whilst your body rests by me, as I die.

…

Steam Train

On the train to somewhere,
Thoughts left behind in a pool of empty wine,
Slurped down by a bruised and thirsty heart
Maimed by confusion,
Troubled by care departed,
Cheers on the soul by the side lines of love.

The wheels screech on in repeated motion, trundling to their
next destination,
Oh! The tired, troubled train of old is running out of steam,
It's cold carriage cup yearning to be filled with light,
laughter and love.

…

Spirit

In the stillness of the night
As the clock strikes its watchful hour,
My dreams take hopeful flight
Like a flock of birds singing past the love spire.

The heart falls East
As a cascade of flowing dreams
Into the loving arms of the soul outstretched, where hope
once lay deceased.

Buried was the mind, whose hostage took the body
Then washed it clean,
Propped up against the tomb-grave of hope, untangled and
laid out to rest, in peace.

...

The Gas-Lit Stone Wall

Leaning against the cold stone wall,
Gas light hissing, yelling I'm home!
No questions answered and silent is the air
That falls on the gently rocking boats below,
Bobbing and dancing to a secret knowing.

I wasn't really there,
It was all in my mind,
Even the gas light didn't hiss;
There was no stone wall
Because no one heard the rap on the door.

…

Coventry

Coventry, oh Coventry! That familiar place,
Where I reside so cosily alongside that old face
Where the bells chime to start the sound of your silence
now,
The classroom is dulled; I didn't know the row.

Crumpled up notes threw odd sense around,
That beautiful old clock-face didn't dare make a sound
In the city of Coventry, to where bad souls are sent,
In your late-night casino, not an honest coin is spent.

…

Hope

Thank you for delivering when my faith was lost,
Leaves turned grey and heart had cost.
Career in tatters, hopes in shreds,
Like a roaming bag lady playing musical beds.

The sun hadn't shone for a very long time,
Death round the corner, when would the clock chime?
Hungry for safety, thirsty for peace,
Searching for affirmation to deal with my grief.

The giving, the unknowing, the grim reality of fear,
For the person you loved wouldn't come very near.
Whilst living the day a ghost roamed the back yard,
You never realised life could be this hard.

Until out of the blue, heart on the ground,
Came a shimmer of hope so I turned around.
The sun's light was stepping out from behind the black
cloud,
My heart filled with joy and sang out aloud.

...

Love

Love lives within us, it never leaves,
Not whilst lying by jealousy or playing with greed.
It transcends this Earth, spirit afar, can shatter me to pieces,
A kaleidoscope of stars.

In a single breath, the word lays plain
It's inherent nature to challenge our gain.
The light falls on our friends before us, that is love,
The joy from the giving,
Paints the blue skies above.

…

Waiting

Woohoohoo! I'm tickety boo,
The train's rolling in and I'm waiting for you.
It's been too long, can't believe you'll be here,
My face runs a river with all the fresh tears.

We've talk-walked this moment, many a time,
Aching to know when that clock's gonna chime.
Dreams have played over like a film in my head,
And the heart's pumping overspill, way-which to tread?

The train pulls in, wheels sleek, but screech slow,
It stops and the doors bang the sides as they go.
Which carriage? I ask as my breath smokes the air,
I daren't look up for the answer to my prayers.

The heart skips a beat, then drains out in cold,
I spin round on my heels coz there's nowhere to go.
The train chants on forward, no message in its song,
The darkness falls down, in a second it's just gone.

Then a voice from behind me, softly resonates my deaf ears,
  As if it were yesterday, though it's been thirty years.
  I see your blue eyes swimming through my wet face,
  Once frozen, now melted, in your tender embrace.

...

Low

Flying low in your mind,
Clumps of sordid gravel spray the tarnished floor
Where underneath the mulch of shattered dreams your soul
hangs out to dry, unfulfilled and grimy.

Where hope once was, but now is
Lost to the chaotic world bought at the highest price,
Expectant of dreamy sights, ambitions' delight,
Regretfully abandoned, but reminded in full hearts.

Where dancing across that weakened eye or upon your
weeping tear,
Evaporated and inhaled by grey skies it does reside,
'Til tides wash away the stolen pride
Banged up with the rest behind strong bars.

Who knew your name, what you did to task in mind?
The souls of who flew alongside your wings of shame, those
who reminded you of who you were,

Take a chance or a penny and spend it how you would,
You're still the same.

…

Misunderstood

Hell's broken loose, watered face in flames,
Ran out o' the end door, just to start once again,
Spittle angry and foaming from the mouth,
Walls closing in, I can't hear myself shout.

Transported to another realm I now see,
The sudden culmination of my own history,
Voiceful and resonant, eclipsing my deaf ears,
Dividing my heart and blessing my hurt tears.

…

No Good

You are no good, I told you so
As good as a rake, or just a garden hoe
That gets up the weeds
And who knows what, am I more I ask, or is it just that?

...

Strong

I love a good foil, I need a good wall,
One wraps you up; the other protects a fall,
Bake my sheets well and strong,
Protect me from what's coming on,
For who knows what lies ahead,
I'll cook my head in soft dough bread.

…

OCD

Take me off to a far-flung place,
To sit with my mind,
Against the bark of a tree, and let nature be kind.

Too much thinking,
Not good for the soul,
Repetitive and guilty,
With no healthy goal.

So I'll embrace this tree,
And sit very still,
Feel the energy flow through
And try to settle my will.

...

Dear Dream

It feels like an age since we first met,
And time has wandered through time.
My stomach turns on itself like a frightened teenager who
knows not what the thought of him does.
Intimate addict, we share,
Though I know we can only be friends.
My heart is dancing, yet sorrowful,
This is the way it always will be
Through time uninterrupted,
Save when you smile at me through the warm dim light,
Whose gaze hits the side of your face, masterfully carving
your jaw.
Your eyes melt my heart when they smile through long
lashes of love,
You've brought me back from the grave of indifference, the
years of hopeless trying to save another,
If only you knew how you felt in my tender heart
Pierced by the tears of too much knowing, fallen upon the
stale ideals of the past.

…

Where Has All the Love Gone?

Where has all the love gone?
It's disappeared, it seems to me,
Stars that shone bright
Now the tarnished hue upon an urn of tears,
Opaque and obscured from the dark night sky,
Wept and drained down past the years.

I've turned up every sun-scorched pebble,
Searched behind every wave-crest
But can't find you there,
Why are you hiding from me?
Like the swaying flicker of a boat's beacon light,
Sinking down behind the sea's burning line.

Your open arms I cherished bare,
They carried me from here to where?
Now tangled up in the sails of hope
And twisted round the heart's rotting mast.
Meet on Ferry Lane if you wish to stop on by,
I'll sit quietly and wait for you there.

...

43

Another year has been, now past,
The hopes and dreams that meant to last
Are riding down the river's stream,
Tide rising-falling, none left the trees in green.

Child runs down winter river's path,
His rose-cold cheeks shine silky as glass,
How will his hopeful future cry
To larks and starlings that kiss the sky?

…

Gold

All that glitters isn't gold,
Now there's a truth that will unfold,
Behind the silk 'twas tightly spun,
The smoking barrel of a gun.

…

Red Lights

Those lustrous eyes that hid many lies
Wandered down the red-lit street.
Shifty, from side to side,
Rolling and dancing as if to a tide.
Confidently they swooshed and swayed
Picking up the next seed,
Or settled on Robin's breast, but took no heed.

Down the zip wire that bird did fall,
Electric out of the sky.
Upon a stick of delight, started to feed,
Those watchful eyes, furtive indeed.
Under their lids they hid,
During the days that passed.
As if in a slumber and ambivalent to crave,
Where home shone dull in the heart's grave.

…

Alone

The heavy and thick blanket of darkness
Gently drops down upon me,
Closing in, folding in like the enveloping of time.

The mast's light falls dim above me
And all I can hear is the tap, tap, tap of the sails' lines,
Gently tinkling to a slight breath of breeze.

The rug I lie under hugs me close
As a friendly metaphor for life connection,
And softly caresses my lone soul.

The stars above me sing their light song
Then kiss themselves to sleep,
For the clouds have moved in and they're now gone.

...

The Bay

Over the ocean's vast bay my gaze swept,
Green glided into blue, returned to green in lines,
Gold sun poured over this blanket like glitter
And the sound of gulls faintly carried from the rocks.

Light off-shore breeze darted over the surface like shoals of
tiny fish,
White puffs of cloud made patterns in transient mood,
A chirping sparrow landed on the sea wall
And the calmness of nature's breath was sound.

...

Waves

Licking their way through the rocks' divides,
Snaking and slithering to the will of the tides, lapping and
slapping the concrete sea wall,
Just to retreat before their next call.

Push-pull and circling the current's new route,
Dancing like fairies to the sound of a lute,
Twirling and whirling they reel in the shore's line,
Living the moment, but stealing its time.

They carry with them the spirit of soul's divine lost,
They pound, beat and slay at war's stubborn cost,
Rising up, hell-bent, in a split second enraged,
Like the blackest of tempers released from its cage.

...

Regatta

White yacht sails dapple the ocean
Like the flick of an artist's brush on canvass,
Spinnakers blow out their balloons in rainbows; a
celebration prelude
While mackerel swim through the sky in hot pursuit.

The sea is burst upon by a majestic explosion of colour,
Fishermen's nets drape over sea walls in a mesh of twisted
bunting, their depths lined with glistening starfish,
Red Arrows twist and turn in thunderous claps of smoke.

Sticks of coloured rock are stuck to the mouths of youth,
Coconuts pop off in shies, smiles abound, voices boom
through megaphones and rowers stride in eights.

Cobbled streets carry the voices of merry men
Popping through the froth of happy beer,
Hot candy floss, twisted like puffy thread, permeates the air
And seagulls steal ice cream, pecking at old news.

This spectacle comes once only in the year,
Memories distilled like wispy boats in bottles,
Tired-happy bodies sleep in salt-musty sheets
And tales are sent in postcards, shiny, though late.

...

To My Autumn

Ebbing away to a far-flung place
Where skies are cold-bright,
The leaf that falls from russet trees
Dances away from the warm autumn breeze.

The grass turns straw-like, crunchy underfoot,
The sun sets a mellow hue
Of copper and gold, tinted by majesty
And crowned in delight.

Seasonal mists that mellow the fruitful summer
Hover above ground like a silk blanket heaven-sent,
Cloaking the land in loving embrace,
Shielding from cold the Earth's divine grace.

Fallen to slumber this season's departed,
Harvesting the colours just passed,
The leaf turns from green to shimmering gold
And holds in its heart secrets of autumn untold.

...

Broken

There we go again you see,
Chalk that one up to history.
Blinded by the rays of lust,
I missed the trick, left on the cusp.

You see a treat so good to eat,
If ever we really were to meet.
Messy is as messy does,
To break my heart for your true love.

We really shouldn't have strayed so close, inevitable, it
renders my heart morose.
The writing was on the wall, I knew,
But I couldn't help adoring you.

…

From Glasgow

I'm in trouble, I know I am,
Clear the decks and neck the dram.
Dusty bagpipes sound dour repeat,
Swig the dram it tastes so neat.

Traipsing up the mountain far,
Tail droops low, legs bent, ajar.
My slovenly gait in truest need,
I knewest now my heart was deed.

…

Escape

Through the wired gauze of my hutch I now see, the way my
life since, has been looking for me.
Enslaved within my battered run,
Forgotten, that my time might now have come.

Dreaming headily of a life outside,
My heart thumps loud with the tail of the ride.
The paw beneath the straw afoot,
Revved-up and ready, a chance, I look.

Grass smells green and sky tastes bold,
I leap and run to escape the old.
The life that held me embittered, so mean,
Be watchful not to act so keen.

The shrub I see is my horizon now,
Heart palpitating, I wipe my brow.
For if my fitness leaves me for my age.
I'll be snatched up and put back in my cage.

...

Untitled

What is your name boy,
Is it blue, or is it green,
How do you spend your days boy,
Are you banging on the scene?

Where are you now love,
Did you think it was all a laugh,
Did you realise at the time boy,
You were cutting your days in half?

Did you see a future full of roses
Just sitting by the sea,
Your mummy's making cakes boy
And you're sipping cups of tea?

Did death get too much love,
Were you angry and confused,
Nowhere to turn to
So it's buried in a bag of blues?

The strangest thing about this all
Is you'd just laid down your friend,
But little did you know
You were coming to your own end.

The funeral was hard mate
The worst that I've yet done,
But your head lies in the hills love and your feet are in the
sun.

...

Meet

Twisting lips divide the rocks
And my misty glare is calling for thee, cast beyond the
headland from the distant trees
The melody of time so near has drawn me close.

I can feel the embrace that's calling,
Upon the chance of hour my soul cannot rest until it's met
with thee, in silent closeness together we will hold our
dreams of distant time where in our memories we were
mine.

...

Poppy Flower

She sits in her serenity amidst a pulsing of sensual colour;
delicate to touch, blooming headily, sequentially, and
dancing in the sun.

Pick her from the earth and she will wither quickly;
her efflorescence, intoxicating, but transitory.

Water her stem for all that is to nurture. The mother of wild
fields;
A symbol of remembrance for the blood of those
never forgotten.

...

Prayer

It's my life,
I'll live it my way
In the best way I know how,
For there'll be nothing to take with us when we go, except
nourished love.
Not the money, the status or the power, but our contribution
to humanity in the kindness that we showed.
My hopes and dreams,
Some realised and some abandoned,
Through trials and triumphs,
When I close my eyes for the last time
I'll be happy to have honoured God.

…

Wounded Wisdom

Where the moon shines, fall the wounded tears upon the
water,
Shimmering with the wisdom and hope of days past,
Come riseth! To the surface with renewed hope and glory,
Forgotten, therein lay the pains of your beaten soul.

Rise again, up against the tides of conflict,
Sink thine oar down in choppy waters thence,
For you will reach the peak of your own mountain,
The voyage beyond your lonely plight to return home.

...